Dead or In Prison

My Journey through Foster Care

By
George E. Duvall
With
Derek D. Humfleet

EAST SIDE

PROJECTS LLC

ISBN 978-0-9903141-0-3
ISBN 978-0-9903141-1-0 (electronic)

Cover design and photographs by Crimson Duvall.

For more information about George Duvall, visit
www.georgeduvallspeaks.com.

For more information about East Side Projects, LLC
visit www.eastsideprojectsllc.com.

Contents

Dedication

From George »

This book is dedicated to my kids, Sienna, Jaycee and Cyan, who will most likely never see the Foster Care system. I also dedicate this book to my wife Crimson who also made sure our kids will not see the Foster Care system. She also took the cover and back photos of my book. This book is also dedicated to my Foster Family (My Family), Melanie and Greg Harris, Larry and Monqwae'el Scott and my Cousin Nikki Hines. No matter what, we all stuck through it all and continue to do so.

To the Foster Parents and Social workers, no matter what a young person say's to you, they need you! You all will make a difference in a young person's Life! Who knows, maybe the next book written will be written by a former youth who you inspired!

My last dedication goes out to the Youth in the Foster Care system. The first chapter of your book of Life was not written by you. But, how your book of Life ends is up to you! Remember, I was told I was going to be "Dead or in Prison" and now I'm an Author! "Believe and you will achieve!"

From Derek »

To my wife, Angie, I still can't believe you said yes. To my boys, Griffin and Colt, you keep me on my toes. To my parents, Joann and Deverle, thank you for your patience in raising me to be the man I am. To George, for letting me dive into your life. To Foster Parents, for all you do for children with stories like George. And to the Lord above, thanks new grace every day.

Preface
Dead or In Prison

I was 7 years old. "You will be dead or in prison by the time you're 13." It was my uncle. He was talking about me. I was a thief. I robbed people. I didn't care. I was a bad kid. At the time, his words were true.

It was the summer of 1982. I was one of five kids. I didn't have a father at home.

I lived in the projects on the east side of Lexington. I clearly remember the day it happened, the day my uncle told me I would be "dead or in prison." It was a Friday night, almost dusk. I wanted to go to my grandparents' house and they lived about two miles away. Along that path I would pass drug dealers, thieves, thugs, players and pretenders. These were my father figures. I was their entertainment.

They liked me. I was a "Hard Lil' Nigga!" Their boom boxes rocked 80's rap. I would dance for them. I made *them* laugh. They made *me* promises. I was going to be "the man" one day. I could flash my broad smile with the gap between my front teeth and they gave me dollar food stamps. They were cool. They gave me attention. They built a relationship with me. I listened to them. They were my examples.

Food stamps meant I could buy candy; Boston Bake Beans, Lemon Heads, Chick-O-Sticks and my favorite, Now & Laters. That night I stopped at the store on the corner of Fourth and Ohio Streets. I used the food stamps my "fathers" gave me and loaded up on candy. Then I was off to my Grandparents' house.

I loved their house. I was the youngest grandchild. This entitled me to special attention. Even at the young age of seven I was already getting into a lot of trouble. But, I was also a hard worker. I helped them out even when they didn't ask, in order to earn their special attention. Attention was my drug. It was what I *craved*. I didn't get much attention at home.

My grandparents were great people. Grandmamma only stood about four foot eleven. She cooked. She cleaned. She kept the house nice. For a while, she was even a preacher. Grandmamma read the Bible to me. She told me I was beautiful. My Granddaddy was a big man. He took his Second Amendment rights seriously. If you crossed him he was not afraid to straighten you out. He talked to me. He listened to me. He cared about what I thought. Neither of my grandparents took any insubordination from either their kids or grandkids, myself included.

That night, when I finally I got to their house, I opened the wrought iron gate and yelled for Grandmamma like a celebrity announcing his appearance. She didn't hear me so I let myself in.

When I walked in the door I saw my uncle. He was passed out, face down in the middle of the living room floor, snoring.

He was probably twenty-five years old and he worked for a living. Friday was payday, so he had picked up a bottle of liquor after he got off work. His wallet was sticking out of his pants. It had a chain connecting it to his belt. In his drunkenness, he snored and snored and snored some more. I saw this as an opportunity. I waited, watched and listened. I tiptoed across the linoleum to where he was sleeping. I slowly bent over him and gently tugged at the leather wallet in his back right side pocket. I almost had it.

Suddenly there was a violent swing! My uncle reached for his wallet, but instead he grabbed my wrist.

Oh boy!

I yelled, "GRANDMAMMA!" and she came running into the living room. There she saw my six foot three inch uncle whoopin' on me.

He shouted, in his Mississippi drawl, "You ain't no good boy!"

He hit me on my back, on my leg, on my butt, and on my hip; whatever he could hit as I tried to jump away. With each swing he was yellin' at me.

"Keep doin' this here! (Whop!) Keep on doin' this, you hear me! (Whop!) You too old for your age boy! (Whop!)"

I could see the anger, the frustration, and most of all, the disappointment in his eyes.

"Keep on George! (Whop!) Keep on doin' this and you will be dead or in prison by the time you're 13!" (Whop! Whop! Whop!)

Then I heard a powerful voice. "Put my baby down, James!"

I had often heard that voice when I got in trouble, but now it was like a voice from Heaven. "I *said* put my baby down, James!"

Because my uncle was so drunk and upset with me, he began cursing at Grandmamma. "Yeah Momma, this little mother-fucker here is going to prison! He just tried to take my wallet, Momma! Yeah, dead or in prison for sure for this little mother-fucker!"

I couldn't look at either one of them.

I heard another "Whop!" but this time I didn't feel anything. I turned around and saw my little grandmamma jump in the air like Michael Jordan and smack the taste out of James' mouth. Now, most of my family would say she smacked him for cussing around her like he did, but I would say she did it because I was her favorite grandson, and I was just seven years old.

She forced my uncle to back down. He was still furious and drunk. About that time my granddaddy walked in the living room. He saw that Grandmamma was shielding me from James. When he saw what was happening. He calmly went to his bedroom. My uncle was still pacing and fuming until Granddaddy walked out of his bedroom carrying a double barrel shotgun. My uncle calmed down. Grandmamma did not. For the next thirty minutes my grandmamma preached to my uncle. She preached to him about drinking. She preached to him about fighting. She preached to him about respect. Granddaddy sat on the couch with his double barrel shotgun, just in case Uncle James didn't get the message.

After the sermon was over Grandmamma took me back to her kitchen. There she could feed me, calm me down, and help me relax. It also gave my uncle, who was still intoxicated, time to pass back out.

She and my granddaddy had magic powers over me when I was around them. My bad behavior drifted away. I didn't need to rob, to steal, to fight or impress anyone when I was around them. I was safe there. I knew when I needed a safe place I could go to my grandparents' house. When I was with them I knew I would not be "dead or in prison."

Granddaddy taught me a love of fishing. One day when we were out fishing, Granddaddy asked "Do you know who your 'real' father is?"

At the time I thought it was the guy who lived at our house.

Granddaddy seemed upset with my answer. He said "No! The man staying in your home is a good man, but your father lives around the corner from our house. Let's walk."

As we walked I knew he had something on his mind. He kept me engaged in conversation by telling me stories. He told me stories of growing up in Mississippi and how he met my grandmamma in Cuba, Alabama. He was a confident man and he valued me.

We arrived at an old worn down apartment complex. I passed this place every time I walked from my house to theirs.

We walked up to one of the doors.

He knocked.

A man came to the door. He showed the utmost respect to my granddaddy.

I kept silent and waited to see what would happen. They shook hands and Granddaddy whispered something to the man.

This man came toward me. He put out his hand. "Hey, I hear your name is George. My name is George too."

I said, "Yes." I still had my eyes on my Granddaddy.

He looked back at Granddaddy who nodded at him. The man said, "I'm your father."

Granddaddy told the man, "I'm taking my Grandson fishing tomorrow and you are going with us." It wasn't a request.

He said "I have to work."

Granddaddy frowned. "Well, tell your boss it's going to be your last day."

Sometimes Granddaddy could be very persuasive. This was one of those times. He pulled his pistol out of his pocket to get his point across.

The next day my biological father was at my grandparents' door early in the morning with fishing poles and a six pack of grape soda. He knew my Granddaddy liked grape soda.

You see, Granddaddy knew I was starting to get into trouble regularly. He thought I needed a *positive* male role model to help me survive and become a man. Granddaddy was that role model until I made it to the foster care system. There I found other mentors and role models who helped me on my journey through life.

This book is about my journey. My life started on the streets, in poverty, without hope. I was a very bad kid with little hope for a positive future. Foster care changed my life and sent me in a very different and positive direction. It was not always smooth sailing; there were bumps and difficulties all along the way. I spent some of my teenage years, in the late 1980's and early 1990's as a black teenager living with a white family and a predominately white area. Racism was a problem for me, my family, and my friends. But I made it through of the system. I came out of it with a different kind of name for myself.

These stories are all true. Some of the names have been changed to protect the innocent and the guilty. I am not dead, and while I did spend time in jail as a juvenile, I have never been to prison. I hope you enjoy it.

Chapter 1
Growing up in the East Side Projects

Trouble was a part of my life from the beginning. At four-years-old I walked, by myself, from the projects in East Lexington to Woolworth's Department Store. My prime target was the candy from the counter next to the exit. Every Saturday I walked in with empty pockets and walked out with my pockets full of candy.

One day, a young girl who worked there became suspicious. She asked for my name.

I smiled my toothiest smile and said, "George."

She asked where my mother was. Without missing a beat, I said, "Mom is next door at the drug store."

She was smart. She knew I was lying. Her next question was, "What do you have in your pockets?"

I was not prepared. While I was trying to come up with another lie, she put her hand into my pocket and found it full of candy. I was busted. So I did what other four-year-olds do . . . I started crying.

It worked. Instead of calling the police she decided to teach me a lesson. She told me stealing was wrong. If

I wanted something I should work for it. She then had an idea; she would pay me one quarter to pick up all the hangers on the floor of the department store. I could then use that quarter to *buy* some candy.

No one had ever taken the time to explain this to me. For the next few months every Saturday morning I got up and walked to Woolworth's to pick up hangers. I would earn a quarter each week, buy myself some candy, and go back home to the projects.

This young girl, who probably forgot long ago about the four-year-old boy she mentored back at Woolworth's, taught me a life lesson; the value of hard work. Time and time again I've found that when I work hard I stay out of trouble. She was one of the first people outside of the projects who gave me what I craved . . . attention.

Gaining everyone's attention came naturally to me, even at a young age. The older kids saw this and took me under their wings. With no real father figure in my, life these eight-to-sixteen-year-old kids became my mentors.

My biological mother had no real education. She also had to deal with four other kids, two of whom were mentally challenged. So her time and influence was very limited. I love her. I know she did all that she could for me. However, she was trapped in a cycle of poverty. No one wanted to help her escape; no one wanted to give her a hand up. We were known as the *poorest* family on welfare, even though *everyone* in the projects was on welfare. With our family at the bottom, every other family had someone they could look down on and say, "At least we aren't them."

My physical features made it easy for other kids to pick at me. Some kids made fun of the gap in my teeth, others made fun of my big lips. I gravitated away from those kids toward a more troubled group because I was "cool with them." They gave me attention. While the young girl from Woolworth's gave me positive attention, the attention I was getting back home in the projects was not so positive, but at least I belonged to something.

We formed a crew: The Eastside Project Crew. There were six of us; Lenny, Angela, Coo Coo, Shannon Bug, my older brother Kenny and me. They were my family. What they said mattered. What they did mattered. What they didn't do mattered too, they didn't make fun of me, they didn't make fun of my mamma, and they didn't make fun of Kenny, who some of the other kids labeled as "retarded." In fact they used those taunts and name calling from the others to motivate me.

By the time I was six-years-old I had a reputation for causing trouble. One by one I was kicked out of *all* the elementary schools I attended.

I robbed the teachers.

I robbed the students.

I robbed the elderly.

I stole from grocery stores.

I even stole money from purses and coats during a funeral. - And I *didn't care.*

I was placed in a juvenile detention facility several times. Whenever I got out, my crew would be there for me, telling me how great I was. We would re-live the event and they would say, "Man, George, did you see how fast you ran?" or "George, you told that store owner to fuck off! That was real!"

They were excited for me. They respected me. It was attention and it felt good. My mother would be so proud because they were praising my name instead of making fun of me. My confidence grew.

My crew and I hung out at McDonald's until they closed and dumped their leftover hamburgers and cheeseburgers. We scooped them up after they threw them in the trash, took them to the local bus stop and sold those garbage burgers to unsuspecting passengers.

By the time I was seven, I was uncontrollable. I did whatever I could to gain attention. Attention I wasn't getting from a father. Attention my mother struggled to provide. I also knew I had to put food on the table. Sometimes those garbage burgers came home with me. My family had to eat. The money I was stealing, some of it went to put food on our table. The money I made selling stolen newspapers; it helped my family survive. If there was nothing to eat in the house I would go to the store and steal a roll of bologna, a jar of Miracle Whip and a loaf of bread. I was the provider.

At seven I was independent and feared no one. My body was beginning to develop because my stepfather, who had retired from the military, taught me how to do pushups. I got to where I could do three hundred at a time. He also taught me to box.

One day, after my older brother had hit a girl at school, my stepfather got angry. He told my brother instead of hitting girls, he should be boxing with me. He handed each of us one boxing glove and showed us how to fight. The first match ended when I punched him in the gut. With boxing, I learned about physical pain, how to take it and how to dish it out. As a result, my confidence began to grow. And I don't think my older brother ever hit another girl.

I also had speed and quickness on my side. I was the fastest kid in the neighborhood. I could outrun cops, adults, and teachers or crack-heads, drug dealers, and thugs on bikes.

With my confidence, I challenged older kids and usually won. Once, when I was at the Duncan Park pool, two big thugs smacked me in the face and made fun of my brother and sister.

Anger started building. Others kids were laughing.

Anger kept building. Their taunts reminded me of my past.

Anger kept building. I drew back my right hand, balled my fist up and POW! I popped the one who hit me.

Then I ran. Both of them ran after me and jumped on their bikes. They were yelling "Stop you mu-fuckca!

We're gonna kick yo ass Duvall!" But I didn't stop. I ran toward my house. They couldn't catch me.

When I was about a block away from my house I started yelling "Mamma!" By the time I reached the gate my Stepfather, hearing my cries, stepped out onto the front porch.

I opened the gate, ran up the stairs with tears in my eyes just as the two thugs entered. They began yelling and shouting at me as I tried to explain what happened.

My Stepfather looked at me and asked, "Why are you running?"

The two thugs were still standing at my gate yelling and screaming about how they were gonna 'kick my ass.'

My stepfather said, "You shouldn't run from no one or nothing, no matter how many there are or how bad the situation is."

Then he looked me in the eyes as he held my arms together and told me, "If you don't fight them now, you will be running for the rest of your life."

My tears were replaced with anger and rage, my fear was replaced with courage and determination.

As I walked down the stairs my heart began beating like a drum. I was about to face the kid who had tormented my family and me for years.

I will run no more! Kept going through my head.

Once I reached the small patch of grass in front of our house – POW! He hit me.

I grabbed him and put him in a headlock like I saw the big wrestlers do on Saturday morning wrestling. I held his head and punched him in the face, multiple times. His friend stood on the other side of me and tried to kick me.

I didn't feel it and I didn't let go.

I kept asking him, "You gonna leave me alone? You gonna leave me alone now?"

His eyes turned red.

Finally, I heard "Yes!"

I choked him harder. "What did you say?"

I wanted my Stepfather, who was on the porch, to hear.

He said, "Yes, I will leave you alone. Let me go!"

It was over.

I saw my tormentor later the same month, at the same pool where it all started. This time it was different. When I got out of the pool, he ignored me. It felt good. I left the pool later that day feeling ready to face anything.

On my way home, I decided I would not run any more. Instead, I would fight.

At first I was mad at my Stepfather; he made me fight instead of running off the bullies chasing me. Later I realized his actions gave me the confidence to stand up to anyone at any time, no matter what the outcome. It is a lesson I have carried throughout my life.

By the end of the year I was one of the most recognized kids in the projects. Everyone knew I was a "Duvall." Everyone knew I was trouble. I had what I had always craved, attention. I fought with other crews across Lexington. Whether it was the West Side gangs from Charlotte Court or the Dirty Dirt Bunch from the East Side, I was ready to fight.

My call to arms was, "You don't know me!"

Or "You don't know my crew!"

I didn't care if I got in trouble and it showed. It showed when I was in first grade as I was kicked out of elementary school after elementary school. It showed in facing judge after judge after judge in Juvenile court.

I went from stealing candy at Woolworth's to robbing people as they walked down the road. I usually targeted the weak: older senior citizens who just received their check at the first of the month.

I would snatch their purses, knowing they couldn't catch me. I stole food from Kroger's. I stole toys and clothes from Hill's Department Store and K-Mart.

On Sunday mornings I would take seventy five cents and go to the newspaper rack and take every paper, selling them door to door.

I snuck into the Kentucky Theater to see free movies, sometimes pornography. I was 7 or 8 years old the first time I saw a pornographic movie. I had no father to teach me about relationships or sex or where babies came from; I took what I could get.

Then came the worst crime I ever committed...

My crew and I were at an arcade in downtown Lexington. It was the first of the month and I had stolen some money from my biological mom so we could play games.

We saw a young man roll in and head over to pay Pac-Man. He made the mistake of pulling out a fistful of dollars in order to get change. When we saw that money, my crew and I huddled up to form a plan. I knew I could buy some food with that money. I would not have to go to McDonald's and wait for them to throw out the leftovers so my family and I could eat that night. It was all the motivation I needed.

The oldest kid in my crew suggested I be the one to take the money because I was a lot faster than the others. I agreed. Then I watched and waited for just the right opportunity. My opportunity came when the young man moved away from the Pac-Man machine to another game near the exit. He had no idea what was about to happen. Neither did I. I ran at him in a mad rage, knocked him over, and took his money. Then I ran out the door.

I knew he would not chase after me. He couldn't because he was in a wheelchair.

At the time I did not understand, or care about, what it meant to be in a wheelchair. I was eight years old and all I wanted was to eat and play video games. In retrospect, I am embarrassed by my actions. To this day, I think about how that young man must have felt. For me, this event changed the course of my life.

After the robbery one of my "friends" ratted me out. After I was arrested I was sent, once again, before a juvenile court judge. He knew my mother and me very well. I had been before him many times and my mother had gotten away with many warnings.

The last time we stood before him he specifically told my mother, "I better not see him in my courtroom anymore!"

But he did. On that day in his courtroom, I could feel something different, something serious was about to happen.

The judge didn't hold back. He said my mother was unfit to be a parent. He said I was an uncontrollable kid with behavior problems. He told us his only alternative was to place me in foster care. I did not understand exactly what he meant; I had been taken

away from my mother before, but I was always sent back home.

This time I would not be returning.

My mother started to cry. A large man in a police uniform ushered me away from my mother and took me deep into the bowels of the courthouse to a holding cell. From there I was taken to the Fayette County Juvenile Detention Center. I was an eight-year-old inmate. And this was a facility for teens.

It was my entry into the foster care system.

Luckily, behind the scenes, someone was looking out for me.* She was a powerful woman. She made phone calls to all the Powers That Be, arguing about how it was inappropriate to hold an eight-year-old boy in a teenage detention center.

Her efforts paid off. The next day I went to a temporary foster home. The home was only a couple

---

* There is one person who has always been involved in my life. She is my Angel and I will talk more about her later.

of blocks away from my mother, brothers, and sisters. I thought I was home free, that I had outsmarted the system once again. Little did I know, plans were in the works to send me to a facility designed for young kids with behavior problems...

Chapter 2
Bluegrass Boys' Ranch

The Bluegrass Boys' Ranch was…a ranch.

Located on the outskirts of Lexington, Kentucky, The Bluegrass Boys' Ranch consisted of about 40 acres of tobacco fields, strawberry fields, cattle pasture, hay fields, and an old black barn. The only ranch this inner-city black kid had ever known was the "ranch" salad dressing. This ranch was way out in the country. Big trees hovered over the winding road. I had never seen so much green. As for the people at The Ranch, they had no idea who had just arrived.

I was the youngest boy ever at The Ranch. Bobby, a white man with red hair, was the director of The Ranch. He was in his late 30's to early 40's. Bobby loved kids and must have had the patience of Job.* Papp, his father, was rugged looking and tough skinned. You could tell he was a farmer. Bobby, Papp, and several young boys were waiting on me when I arrived. The youngest one showed me to my room. It was enormous!

---

* The Book of Job is contained in The Bible's Old Testament. He had A LOT of patience.

15

The apartment I grew up in had less than 800 square feet of living space, with six people living there. This room was about three quarters the size of the entire apartment in the housing projects I grew up in. I, along with nine other boys, slept in this huge room on bunk beds. I was impressed with its size.

After I got settled in I had to show them exactly who I was and what I was about.

So I chose one of the older kids, a boy about fifteen or sixteen years old, and started pickin' on him. I was really getting under his skin and he finally punched me in the mouth.

I punched him back and ran toward the kitchen.

He was chasing me.

I grabbed a butcher knife as I ran through the kitchen and out the back door into the back yard. I was ready to use it.

Then I saw Bobby coming at me with his tongue folded underneath his teeth and red spots on his face. His jaw was clenched in anger as he yelled, "GIVE ME THE KNIFE! RIGHT! NOW! GEORGE! GIVE ME THE KNIFE!"

Suddenly, I was experiencing a new emotion. My heart was pounding. My head was aching. Tears started rolling down my face. I was *scared*.

My hands were shaking as I handed Bobby the knife. He passed it to Papp.

Quickly, almost supernaturally, Bobby's anger evaporated and was replaced by a gentle calming voice. In soothing tones he assured me everything was going to be ok. However, he told me our actions have consequences, and I would be punished, but he was not mad. This experience was so foreign to me, an adult male who genuinely seemed to care for me. Later, I went to the older kid's room and apologized.

That night I cried myself to sleep as I thought about my mama, my brothers, and my sisters. They were only a few miles away in the projects of Lexington, but it seemed like I was a whole world away from them, far from the only life I had ever known. Even though I was surrounded by people, for the first time in my life, I felt alone.

Growin' up in the projects of East Lexington I learned the art of the "hustle" and how to survive in an urban environment. At The Ranch, I learned the value of physical labor.

We planted and picked strawberries. We fed cattle. We planted, hoed, topped, cut and stripped tobacco. We hauled hay. *I loved it.* Bobby, Papp and the other boys were always praising my work ethic. It was the attention I needed. When motivated, I worked even harder. They respected me. I felt like a winner.

I grew to love The Ranch. My behavior improved. My confidence grew. I was back in school as a third grader. I made friends at The Ranch and at school. I dreamed of a future that didn't involve welfare, drugs, violence, or prison.

I remember my first Christmas at The Ranch. Anita Madden, who was a well-known business woman and community activist in Lexington, made sure every kid at The Ranch received multiple Christmas gifts; toys, books, clothes. I had never gotten more than one gift for Christmas in my life.

I thought I was the richest kid on earth.

I started excelling in elementary school. Back in the projects I was always a troublemaker. I received more spankings* than I care to remember and rarely got to play during recess. I was the problem student.

---

* Yes spankings. There was no "time-out" when I was a kid. You were lucky if you didn't get knocked out.

I remember one time, before I arrived at The Ranch, one of my many first grade teachers told me to stay in the classroom and sit at my desk while everyone else went to recess. "George," she said, "you better not move from your seat." Then she left. Bad mistake. As soon as she was gone, I took all of the pencils from all of the other desks and put them in my desk.

As I walked by the teacher's desk, I found her purse. And there was money inside it. I took the money and put it with the pencils, knowing she would never figure out what happened. Upon their return from recess the students could not find their pencils. One by one all eyes focused on me. Once again, I was busted. I was told not to return to school for several days.

In some ways, I was very blessed as a kid. Even at my worst moments, I could always find an adult I could cling to for support. When I was younger it was my Angel. As I got older, it was my fourth grade teacher Mrs. Evans.

I passed the third grade while at The Ranch and I looked forward to starting in Mrs. Evans' class. She was like a mother figure. She was very strict and discipline oriented, but also educated and loving at the same time. She warned me, in a warm and caring way, that she would not tolerate my acting out. She often spoke to me with love, discipline, and laughter all at the same time. I think I made an impression on her too.

While in the fourth grade I found a friend, Larry Parks. Larry and I were the toast of the class. We were both outgoing and the girls loved us.

Together, Larry and I gave Mrs. Evans plenty of headaches throughout the year. To her credit, she stood her ground with us. But there was one time when she lost her cool. That is when I learned about empathy.

In 1986 the Space Shuttle, Challenger, exploded shortly after its launch. Christa McAuliffe was on board. She was chosen to be the first teacher ever to go into outer space. Instead, Ms. McAuliffe, and the six other crew members, died during the explosion. It was a tragedy.

When the news broke I could see the heartbreak in Mrs. Evans' face. I could hear the disappointment in her voice that day. At nine-years-old I didn't know how deeply this tragedy affected her or the other teachers.

Growing up, in the wake of tragedy, I found that I could usually make people smile with a quick joke, but this time it backfired horribly. I had heard one of the older kids tell a joke earlier in the day so I repeated it during class to see if I could get the rest of my classmates to laugh.

Of course I told it to Larry first. I asked him, "What does NASA mean?"

"What?" Larry replied.

"Need Another Seven Astronauts!" We both busted out laughing.

Mrs. Evans overheard us.

She asked me to tell the joke to the entire class. I was hesitant. She said "George, Larry, you want to tell the class what's so funny?" I said "No." She was insistent, so I told the joke.

No one else found it funny.

I was sent to the principal's office. The next thing I knew, Bobby was there to pick me up. On the way back to The Ranch he explained why Mrs. Evans was so upset and why my joke got me into trouble. I felt horrible. I had upset Mrs. Evans. Given my troubled past I never wanted to make adults who cared for me upset.

Bobby told me what I should do to make up for the joke. So, the next day I apologized to Mrs. Evans. She accepted my apology and explained why she felt the way she did and what this tragedy meant to my teachers.

Mrs. Evans gave me something intangible, something I needed, something I wanted: hope and empathy.

We had other speed bumps in the fourth grade.

I called another teacher a "bitch" claiming I was reading the dictionary. I stunk up the entire fourth grade class when I used a whole bottle of Polo cologne I had stolen from one of the older boys at The Ranch.

Even after all my shenanigans, Mrs. Evans looked past my immaturity and invited me into her home for cookouts. I met her family. I made them laugh. They treated me like I was any other kid, not a troublemaker from the projects of East Lexington.

She loved me. She came to see me graduate from high school in Northern Kentucky. I guess she had to see it for herself.

My behavior improved while I was at The Ranch, but when I went home to visit, I fell into the same old habits.* While visiting my mother I was able to reconnect with my crew. We would stay up late and just hang out. At least now I didn't have any major run-ins with the police. But something had changed. I had discovered other, more positive, ways to get attention.

In the middle of my second year at The Ranch I was told I would be returning home to my biological family due to my behavioral progress. I was stunned. This news felt like a punch to the gut, only this punch didn't get better.

For me, returning home meant returning to the projects, welfare, and shattered dreams. I had found peace and sanctuary at The Ranch. Any time I was having problems or anxiety I could go to my castle in the big black barn. Neither peace nor sanctuary was available in the projects.

We stacked bales of hay in the barn. I could move the hay around and build a castle. It was my sanctuary. It welcomed me. There were secret chambers only a

---

* Even in the foster care system I returned to my biological family one weekend a month, sometimes more.

small boy could get into. Once in the right position I would imagine the hay surrounding me was the stone fortress of a castle where no problems could reach me.

Sometimes I would move the hay around to make other smaller castles for my family even though they were back in the projects.

My behavior regressed when I found out I may have to go back to the projects. I started acting out again at school and The Ranch.

It all came to a head one Friday afternoon at The Ranch. I did the *unthinkable*.

That Friday most of the boys were on home visits with their families. Bobby and his family took the remaining boys on an outing and I was left at The Ranch by myself waiting for my mother to find a ride to come and get me. I found myself at the barn working on my castles.

It was getting late and I figured my mamma could not find a ride to come pick me up. I started walking back up toward the house when I heard something strange. . . silence.

I walked in and yelled "Bobby? Papp? Is anyone here?"

No answer.

I began to case the joint. I got into Bobby's apartment in The Ranch. I looked around rummaging through Bobby's stuff, that's when I saw it. A small envelop with familiar green paper hanging out the side. Money. In a sleeve, like when you come from a bank.

I tried to ignore it, but it called out my name.

I picked it up and counted it.

It was close to $500!

I thought about all the ways I could spend it. But this was Bobby's money. He was one of the few adults that got me. He understood my reasons for acting out. He protected me from myself. *I couldn't steal from him. It would be the ultimate betrayal of an adult who saw promise in me.* I would love to say I put it back. I didn't.

Next thing I knew I was back in the projects with a pocket full of money.

I bought myself a new bike.

When I returned to The Ranch with my new bike, Bobby knew something was up. I told him my biological father bought it for me. He saw right through my lie. Once again, I was busted.

I found out the money was for a lawyer for some type of legal expense he needed for his family.

My heart sank.

I could see the disappointment in his eyes. I could hear it in his voice.

I could no longer live at The Ranch.

Everything I had grown accustomed to would disappear. I would not return to the class I learned to love. I never got to see Larry again. Though I did get to see Mrs. Evans again, it was years later. It was a painful lesson.

The summer after my fourth grade year I was sent to another boys home . . .90 miles from home.

Chapter 3
90 Miles from Home

My actions at The Ranch changed the trajectory of my life. Although I had made positive steps at The Ranch, I found myself getting ready to move again. I had my garbage bags packed when my social worker* picked me up. I had never seen a social worker like her before. She was young and pretty with long blond hair. It was the summer of 1986. She picked me up in her gold Toyota MR2. I had never seen a car like that before either.

Despite her looks and her car, as she was helping me load my garbage bags, all I could think about was how sorry I was for stealing Bobby's money. What had I done? How could I have been so stupid? Where the hell was I going now?

I didn't talk much as we left the ranch. She didn't either after the first 10 to 15 miles. I sat in the passenger seat of her MR2 watching the Central Kentucky bluegrass pass by.

---

* Years later we would work together on projects for foster children.

Thirty minutes into the trip I finally asked where I was going. She said the Covington Protestant Children's Home in Covington, Kentucky.

With no sense of where Covington, Kentucky was, I sat back and waited . . . and waited . . . and waited.

Until finally, I fell asleep.

The next thing I knew she was pushing on my legs saying "George, George. We're here." I wiped my eyes and thought *Where the hell am I?* as we drove down the wooded road into Devou Park. There were many beautiful houses; one was all brick, one was all glass overlooking the golf course. We passed a museum. I thought maybe this place wasn't so bad.

We entered a straight stretch toward a huge building with beautiful landscape. She parked her gold MR2 near the entrance where a man was standing, waiting for us.

As I got out of the car I asked her, "Where is my mother?" She said, "In Lexington."

"Where is Lexington?" I asked.

She said, "Ninety miles from here."

All I thought about the rest of the night was, *90 miles.*

The man who had been waiting for us grabbed my garbage bags and ushered me into this huge building designed for young boys with behavior problems.

Knowing how far away my mama was made me angry. She could rarely find someone who could drive a few miles to the outskirts of Lexington when I was at The Ranch. How could she find someone to drive 90 miles to pick me up?

Would I ever see my brothers and sisters again?

All these thoughts and more were rushing through my mind as I pulled my belongings from the garbage bags and put them in my room.

The more stuff I put away the more my anger was building. I overheard the staff discussing my prior behavioral issues. Since they knew I was a kid with behavior problems. I wondered what else they knew.

The other boys in the home needed to know who I was and what I was capable of.

It didn't take much. A stray comment from one of the older boys was enough.

POW! I punched him in the face.

We locked up and rolled around on the floor until one of the staff, Patrick, broke up our fight. He grabbed both of us and pulled us apart.

However, I was not ready to quit.

Patrick was used to dealing with punks like me. He used some kind of hand and leg lock and put me in a position where I could not move. I had never seen or felt anything like it. Pat was trained in the martial arts.

I said "Let me up you mother fucker! Let go of me!"*

The more I cursed the tighter it got.

Patrick said "Stop that yelling George. Calm down."

After about six minutes, Patrick wore me down. I stopped cursing because I had to focus on breathing. The anger and rage began to subside.

Patrick slowly released his hold on me. Finally he let go and helped me to my feet. He told me I was not allowed to participate in any activities for the next two days. I wanted to know where this skinny red headed white guy learned his moves.

---

* I was very creative with my words.

Still, all I could think about was my mother, brothers, sisters, and Lexington. Even if I knew I had no future there, I needed to know they were close by and maybe they would be there for me if I needed them.

In foster care I had to change my attitude. It was a slow process. My anger turned to sadness. I missed my family and my crew. I formed a plan. I would adopt a better attitude. There was a school on the campus of The Children's Home. I would work my tail off. I would do whatever it took to get back to my family and my crew in Lexington.

After about six or seven months I began volunteering to work around the facility. Work was something I excelled at and it gave me positive reinforcement.

Whether it was taking out the trash, washing dishes or cleaning up the woodshop I would do it. Once again my grades began to improve.

Other boys and the staff noticed the change. Patrick and I became very close. Whenever I had problems or needed someone to talk to I would go to Patrick.

As our friendship grew closer, other boys asked me for suggestions on how to approach and talk to Patrick. They heard how I came into the home and saw how I changed. Tom Bricking was the director of the Covington Children's Home.

Along with Pat, Tom Bricking, who was the director of the Covington Children's Home, saw I was a leader and talked to me about how I could influence other boys at the home in a positive way. They loved my energy and my smile. I had never heard men talk to me this way. It was like I was a member of their family, their equal. They became father figures in my life.*

The staff talked about how I was stepping up and becoming an example for the other boys. I began feeling good once again. It was all part of my plan . . . to get back home to Mamma, 90 miles away.

There was a program at The Children's Home called "Moving On." Once you were in "Moving On" you were able to leave the home campus on your own for a couple of hours a day several times a week. Due to the changes in my behavior I was able to get into the "Moving On" program.

---

* Since I graduated from college I returned several times to the Covington Children's Home to speak to the current residents and staff. I even applied for a job there.

I was feeling more and more important. The staff trusted me. Pat trusted me. My plan was working. I would get back home. No one was going to stop me. That is, until a special family found me, took me in, and showed me a new kind of love.

The house I lived in, in East Lexington.
It is the scene of my first fight. My stepfather
stood on the porch and watched.
Photos on this page by Crimson Duvall

Our Market. I used to steal from this store
monthly. My biological father lived in the
apartment behind the store.

My first alternative placement,
the Bluegrass Boys' Ranch.

This was my home at the Bluegrass
Boys' Ranch for about a year and a half.

The Barn, at the Bluegrass Boys' Ranch,
where I built my castles.
Photos on this page by Crimson Duvall.

Me, at my Angel's house. When I was there I felt like Superman.

My first trip outside of Kentucky with My Angel's husband.

Chapter 4
Could a White Family Love a
Young Black Teen?

When I entered The Children's Home I was an angry kid with behavioral problems and little discipline. After a year, I was the kid with the positive smile and winning attitude.

At about the same time, The Children's Home began to branch out and include a foster care program servicing Northern Kentucky. Because of my good behavior, I was asked if I wanted to participate. I quickly said yes. . . I saw it as another step in my plan to get back to my family in Lexington.

One of my friends at The Children's Home was "Scooter." We both wanted to get back to our biological homes. He and I would hang out and make plans.

We both saw the foster care program as a step in that direction.

On Sundays, potential foster families had the opportunity to spend time with kids in the foster program. On our first Sunday, Scooter and I put on our finest clothes and our freshest faces.

As interested families toured The Children's Home, we smiled and listened as the tour guides talked about the history of the home. They told the families how great the kids in The Children's home could be... given the right circumstances.

The staff felt foster care was the circumstance necessary to change our lives, so they sold the programs as if they were trying to sell a used car. Scooter and I kind of felt like zoo animals.

The foster care program drew several families from Northern Kentucky.

They would bring their own biological kids to The Children's Home to see how we interacted.

I hit it off with a couple of kids who were close to my age very quickly, Jeff and Abe. Their parents came back several weeks in a row.

When they came to the home they would even ask for me by name. They enjoyed spending time with me. If I knew they were coming, I made sure I was around and very visible.

There was a softball field in front of The Children's Home. We would go out there and play catch. At the home we didn't have bats or gloves so we played open handed.

Eventually they took me to dinner off campus to Frisch's. Frisch's was one of the most popular local restaurants in Northern Kentucky.

I had never heard of it. I didn't know what to order.

Randy, the father, ordered me a Frisch's Big Boy with fries and extra tartar sauce. I asked Randy why we needed extra tartar sauce.

He smiled and told me, "It's for your fries."

Their youngest son shook his head enthusiastically.

I was hesitant at first. But when the Big Boy came it looked like a Big Mac, then I knew I was in for a treat. They were right, the tartar sauce made the fries taste even better. I savored that moment. I knew one day, somehow, some way, I would return to Frisch's.

At the end of the meal Randy asked me if I wanted dessert.

What???!!! No one had *ever* asked me if I wanted dessert.

The only dessert I ever had was what I found in the garbage at the local McDonald's in Lexington. If I was lucky, at the end of the night I could find a warm apple pie mixed in with the burgers in the dumpster.

As I was pondering this unusual question, Randy took it upon himself to order a huge Hot Fudge Sundae. The waitress brought it out. I was speechless, certainly a rarity for me. I saw a square of vanilla ice cream sandwiched between two square brownies, with hot fudge and whipped cream. I scarfed down the entire dessert including the gigantic cherry on top.

From that day forward if Patrick or Tom wanted to reward me or calm me down, we went to Frisch's Big Boy.

After dinner they took me back to The Children's Home. I was blissfully full. They assured me they would be back next week. I told their youngest son goodbye and watched as the entire family loaded up into their car and drove off.

While I felt a strong connection forming, I shrugged it off and reminded myself of my plan to get back to Mamma's house 90 miles away.

The next few weekends were a whirlwind of visits. They would come and pick me up on Saturday mornings and bring me back after lunch.

Then they started bringing me back after dinner.

Then they started picking me up on Fridays.

I would spend the entire weekend with them at their home. They lived on a farm in the Belleview Bottoms, about forty-five minutes away from The Children's Home. They lived in an old farmhouse. There were dark areas in the basement of the home where slaves had been kept. It was a very historic home, but at the same time I felt uneasy knowing the history of what had happened there.

They would take me back to The Children's Home after church and Sunday Brunch. And let me tell you, Sunday Brunch was quiet delectable.

Sonya, the mother, would make sausage-gravy and biscuits. The first Sunday I grabbed three or four biscuits and smothered them with sausage gravy. They laughed good naturedly at me. After watching Randy and their kids I learned to tear the biscuits up and then pour the gravy over them.

As I was eating I thought, *Man, this sure tastes better than a Big Boy.*

They had an old dusty barn on their property. It reminded me of the big black barn at The Ranch. We passed the dusty barn whenever we left. I hoped one day to be able to rebuild my castles for me and my biological family.

One night, as I was drifting off to sleep, a thought popped into my head. *If I stayed out of trouble and did well in school, I may be able to go home in six or seven months.*

My only friend, Scooter, had found a foster family and was no longer at The Children's Home. Maybe if Sonya and Randy became my foster parents we could visit Scooter. Maybe, I could get out of The Children's Home. Then, I would return to my biological family 90 miles away.

I *knew* I was a foster child. So I thought Randy and Sonya couldn't really care about me.

I was black.

I was from the city.

I came from a broken home.

I grew up in the projects.

I was a troublemaker.

Randy and Sonya were too different from me.

They were white

They were from the country.

They grew up in a Christian home.

Their lives were stable.

In my mind they were only in it for the money and the glory of being known as foster parents.

I failed to account for the one thing that transcends color, poverty, crime and behavior problems.

Love.

Chapter 5
My First Foster Family

Soon enough Randy and Sonya brought me into their family as a foster child. I finally felt like I was escaping the chains of poverty, welfare, crime and punishment.

When I entered the foster care system I was a thief, robber and fighter. Now I had developed into a leader, a worker and an example. Fighting and robbing were replaced by video games and fishing.

Randy worked in sheet metal. He was an expert and he loved to work on cars. He asked us boys to help. At first, I was useless; I didn't know what tools were. He would ask me to hand him a crowbar and I would look for a candy bar, but I finally got the hang of it.

However, soon after I arrived at Randy and Sonya's I was blindsided by a problem I never saw coming. It complicated my foster care journey.

My first day at my new elementary school was Martin Luther King, Jr. Day. I was the first African American to attend Kelly Elementary School. I was the only African American child in the community. And I lived with a white family, who had never before experienced discrimination or racism. I was not prepared. Randy and Sonya were not prepared.

No one at The Ranch talked about it. No one at The Children's Home talked about it. My social workers never talked about it. For some strange reason no one thought it would be a problem.

Racism.

Growing up black in a predominately white area.

Dating.

Cultural pride.

Identity.

I would soon face these issues head on. I never planned on blazing a trail, but at the time cross-cultural foster care was in its infancy in Kentucky. While Randy and Sonya loved me, they were not prepared for the challenges of raising an African American teenager in an all-white community.

Don't get me wrong. I knew Randy and Sonya loved me. I didn't think they could, but they did. They were *very* loving parents. I believe they loved and supported me the best way they knew how. Unfortunately they had no cultural diversity training.

They relied on their gut instinct, but their experience was very limited.

I grew up in the city where almost everything was a short walk away. Randy and Sonya lived in the country. There were no local supermarkets or gas stations. Rabbit Hash General Store, the nearest place of business, was about five miles away. It had been around for almost 100 years. There was an old wooden porch that creaked when you walked on it. Some of the boards felt like they would give way when you stepped on them. There were old wooden rocking chairs on the porch, always occupied by old men who would sit around and tell stories about days gone by. As the years went on the fish got bigger and the women got prettier. But the best thing about sitting on the front porch of the general store was the breathtaking view of the Ohio River.

Randy and Sonya did get an education on some of the subtle differences that come with raising an African American child. For instance, one day they ran out of lotion. For most Caucasians, running out of lotion is not a big deal. Not so for black folks. If a black person's skin dries out it begins to chafe and crack. It looks really bad. Anyway, I had just gotten out of the shower and was getting ready to go to the local swimming pool. It was August. There was no lotion. I looked around frantically trying to find something to keep my skin moist. Finally I found something . . .

Vaseline.

I rubbed it all over my body. It felt good. It seemed Vaseline was an acceptable substitute for lotion.

Boy was I wrong.

I didn't know it at the time, but Vaseline draws the heat from the sun and traps it on your body. Did I mention it was August?* And the pool was about five miles away. And we had to walk . . . five miles. What started with a trickle of sweat falling down the back of my neck when I left home turned into a shower of sweat about a quarter of the way there.

Usually I had no trouble walking a few miles, but the heat was suddenly stifling. I was walking with some friends and suddenly I couldn't keep up.

"Y'all going to have to slow down!"

---

* For those of you who have not experienced August in Kentucky it is very hot and very humid. Some days you can cut the humidity with a knife. It is definitely not a dry heat, whatever that means.

"What's with the big rush?"

"Why is my skin boiling?"

As soon as we got to the pool I jumped in.

When I got out of the water, I found that my Vaseline rub down had at least one benefit: I could shake myself dry without using a towel.

From that day on, whenever Sonya went to the store I made sure we had plenty of lotion.

However, other issues surfaced without such an easy fix.

When I showed up at Kelly Elementary School all eyes were on me. Soon after I arrived other kids would make racial jokes at school. I was hurt and confused. I didn't know how to respond. I went to Randy and Sonya looking for answers.

Their response "Don't worry about those stupid people. God will take care of their ignorance."

Their response seemed trite. They didn't realize the emotions that gripped me when other kids, my classmates, called me a "nigger."

I had learned to bury my emotions while in foster care, so I sucked it up and did what Randy and Sonya suggested. I waited for God to take care of them. And I waited. And I waited. I thought if I followed the rules, if I did what I was supposed to do in school, if I went to church on Sundays and Wednesdays, kids would stop calling me a "nigger."

It didn't work that way. In fact it got worse.

I was diagnosed with a Behavior Disorder and Learning Disability. The teacher placed me in the corner during class. I sat at a study desk, with my back to the teacher, so I wouldn't "disrupt" the other students.

At some time during the week when all of the other kids were doing math together in my main classroom, I had to leave to join the other kids who had behavior or learning problems. I did not like this. Randy and Sonya did not stand up for me. They did not speak to my teachers. They did not speak to my principals. They did not investigate whether or not I was truly disabled. It hurt me.

Then girls started coming into the picture.

The first girl I ever "liked" told me "blacks and whites should not be together. The Bible says so."

If anyone knew about the Bible it was Sonya and Randy. So I put the question to them. Randy was unsure. He suggested I be careful with who I talked to or "liked."

I was crushed. I felt like I should suppress my feelings and who I was.

I was mad at myself.

Why did I have to have feelings like that?

Why did I have feelings for a white girl?

What was God doing to me? Why was he punishing me like this?

It got worse.

Other boys were talking about the girls they liked or wanted to "go steady" with.

I couldn't.

What if some white girls' parents found out about my feelings?

What would they think?

More importantly, what would they do?

My whole sixth grade year I looked forward to moving on to junior high school. I had quickly grown tired of being the only black kid at school. I was more than ready to start over at a new school.

I saw it as a new beginning. I would get to spend more time with my new friend, Monqwa'el. I met Qwa'el when I was in the fifth grade. My friend Danny had talked me into playing football with him. Danny and I showed up at the football field. The coach lined us up and told us to sprint down the field. Like I've said earlier, I was fast. I came in first. Qwa'el came in second. We made an instant connection.

It was the beginning of a beautiful friendship.

Chapter 6
Friends Become Brothers

Connor Junior High would never be the same.

I had several classes with Qwa'el. History was the one I remember the most. The teacher knew us because we always sat together, talked and looked at the girls, and somehow always managed to get our work done.

When we first started at Connor, I was still considered a learning disabled student, so I had to leave Qwa'el to go to the "Special Education" class. I hated it. I already had so much attention on me as one of the few black kids at school. These classes made me feel stupid.

I asked the special education teacher if I could be "mainstreamed" back with the regular students. She said I would need to take several tests. I agreed. Then midway through my seventh grade year, I was no longer labeled "learning disabled." I was back with my friend.

As time went on Qwa'el and I became closer. I got to know his family. He had an older brother, Larry. His parents had relocated to Northern Kentucky from

Illinois. They both had good jobs. His mom worked at a local factory and his dad worked for an airline.

Randy and Sonya knew I was longing for a connection to a black family. With the state's permission they would let me spend weekends with Qwa'el and his family. I would go home with Qwa'el after school on Friday's. Randy and Sonya would let me stay until Sunday afternoons, so long as I promised to go to church with Q and his family.

They went to an African American church behind their house. About twelve people regularly attended. Qwa'el's family and I made up five of the twelve regulars.

Qwa'el's family was also good for my hair.

Growing up in East Lexington, barbershops were a cultural necessity. If you wanted to know about the new family moving in down the street, you went to the barber shop. If you wanted to know who was in trouble, you went to the barbershop. If you wanted to know who was dating whom, you went to the barbershop. Of course, if you needed a fresh cut you went to the barbershop too. People would come to the barber shop and stay all day and talk about life, sports, or politics.

There were no barbershops in or near Rural Kentucky. If I wanted a fresh cut I had to wait until I had a home visit back in East Lexington. My childhood barber enjoyed talking to me. I was one of the few kids who could hold an interesting conversation with him.

While he enjoyed the conversation, he hated cutting my hair. My hair was what most people would call nappy. It was never properly maintained and impossible to comb. When I was younger, if Mamma wanted to punish me she would take a fine tooth comb and comb my hair. It was painful. While she was combing my hair, if you were in the same room, you could audibly hear it.

Snap!

Crackle!

Pop!

I remember one time while I was living with Randy and Sonya, I really needed a haircut but I could not get home for several weeks. They had no idea where to take me. So, their youngest son Abe volunteered to cut my hair.

I said "Ok???"

He went downstairs and came back with a cereal bowl and dog shears.

I thought, *Oh. No.* I started to protest, but it was too late.

He put the bowl on my head and went to work.

I heard the dog shears and my hair.

Snap!

Crackle!

Pop!

When he was done I looked in the mirror and

Opened. . .

My. . .

Eyes.

At first my eyes were focused on the floor. My shoes: penny loafers. My pants: tight Levis with the cuffs rolled up tight around my ankles. My shirt: short sleeve, lime green polo shirt. Finally my hair: a bowl cut. I was turning into a geeky white kid.

When Qwa'el and his family saw me they tried to stifle their laughter. I asked them what was the matter and they burst out laughing. After that, Qwa'el's parents started letting Randy and Sonya know when they took their boys to get haircuts. And thankfully, they started asking if I wanted to go along.

Two things Qwa'el and I loved: talking about girls and practicing our dance moves. Qwa'el had a boom box. Bobby Brown's *My Prerogative* was our song. We listened to it on the radio. We watched his video on MTV.

We copied Bobby Brown's dance moves and practiced over and over and over again. We were very good. When it came to the school dances all eyes were on us. One, we could really dance and two, we were token blacks at an all-white school.

At every dance we would go up to the DJ and ask if he had *My Prerogative*. Hip Hop and R & B were not very popular in an all-white community, but if the DJ had it we spread the word; the show was about to begin.

The beat started. The DJ would dedicate the song to us.

"Everybody's talkin all this stuff about me . . . Why don't they just let me live. . ."

It was on. Our moves were so smooth and so slick.

"They say I'm crazy, but I really don't care . . . That's my prerogative."

We went so far as to choreograph our own moves.

We were in sync. Qwa'el's moves, my moves, it was something to behold.

Our dancing entranced teachers as well as students. It brought smiles to their faces. I realized very quickly that girls love a man who can dance. Whenever we got back to Qwa'el's house after a night of dancing, we talked and laughed for hours about who was watching who and whose phone number we got. Life was good.

Two young black teenagers danced their way into the hearts of an all-white community. We were growing up. We were becoming young black men. *Most* of the community loved us.

The Northern Kentucky community was amazing in many ways. But, some students and their parents still hated us . . . because we were different.

It was always difficult for me to understand how people could hate me when they didn't even know me. While I dealt with racist jokes and name calling in elementary school, I came face to face with this type of hatred in the eighth grade.

It was 1990, the first year Martin Luther King, Jr. Day became a national holiday.

On Friday nights my friends and I would go hang out at the mall where we could mix and mingle with other eighth graders, away from school.

This was back when face to face communication was important, especially if you wanted to meet new people. With my background, I always wanted to meet new people. Diversity was important in my life.

After we hung out at the mall for a little while we would go to one of the department stores, douse ourselves in cologne and go to the movie theater across the street.

It was the weekend before MLK day and the word was out that an older white kid was going to "beat the shit outta me" if I showed up at the mall that night. My friends said they wanted to stay at home, watch a movie and eat. They wanted to protect me.

But I was from the East Side of Lexington . . . I didn't back down from threats.

Qwa'el and I, along with Doug and Ian, two of my white friends, went to the mall that evening. We had just finished eating and were headed to the downstairs area of the mall. We were going down the escalator and we saw him. Him and his friends were going up the opposite escalator.

It was like a scene from a movie as we stared each other down, me and my friends going down and him and his friends going up.

We really did not want to start any trouble so we focused on going across the street to the movie theater. As we were leaving the mall, he and his friends caught up with us. Here we were, the only two black teenagers in a predominately white neighborhood, and they were pickin' a fight with us.

I started breathing deeply, taking the maximum amount of oxygen into my lungs with every breath. My nostrils began to flare. Normally I am very talkative, but I grew quiet as I sensed what was coming. This kid did not know he was getting ready to meet the "Gorilla" my Granddaddy created!

This kid was bigger than me.

And he talked . . . a lot.

He talked so much that security heard what was going on and came to break us up . . . while he was still talking.

Luckily -- probably for both of us -- he did not enter my zone of danger.

Before he left he said, "We will finish this at school on Monday."

I just stared at him like Clint Eastwood staring down bad guys in *Dirty Harry*. I wanted to say, "Go ahead. Make my day."

My nostrils were the size of parachutes. My heart was pounding. Anger was seething through my veins. I was so mad I don't remember the movie we saw that night.

Doug's mother picked us up from the theater. I was still mad. I told my friends, "We should have handled it then and there."

On Sunday, Qwa'el and I talked. Since we were African Americans we did not have to go to school on MLK day. I told Qwa'el I would not back down. I was not going to give that kid any reason to gloat. Sleep came reluctantly on Sunday as I anticipated a war.

Monday morning I got up, ate breakfast, got dressed and went to the bus stop. The song *Eye of the Tiger* was playing over and over in my head. There was a serious buzz on the school bus about a fight between me and the other kid. I still didn't understand why he wanted to fight me. I had never done anything to him. I figured it out when the bus pulled into school.

All the white kids were saying, "This should be good." He wanted to fight me just because I was black. Butterflies suddenly punched me in the gut.

I immediately went to the gym hoping to see Qwa'el. He wasn't there. His parents wanted him to stay home because it was MLK day. I turned to walk down the hallway. Other students started following me hoping to catch every moment of the unfolding drama.

That's when I saw him. Our eyes locked. His friends were behind him. No one was behind me. I was alone. We slowly walked toward each other. I kept hoping a teacher would step in.

When we got close he said loud enough for everyone to hear, "What are you doing here on National Nigger Day?"

What.

Did.

He.

Just.

Say?

Everything else was a blur. From that moment on, it was just him and me. Tears were rolling down my face and snot was coming out my nose as I picked him up, turned and power-slammed him to the ground.

No one was ever allowed to call me a "Nigger." I developed an aversion to the "N" word. If you were around me you were not allowed to use the "N" word, even if it was in a song I didn't use it, I replaced the "N" word with "brother." Those who hung around me eventually did the same.

This poor kid caught the unbridled rage of an immature frustrated black kid who grew up poor and more than anything just wanted to be accepted into an all-white community.

The female softball coach tried to separate us, but I was able to shove her off of me. I could not stop until a male basketball coach came and knocked me off of this kid and held me down. It reminded me of the day when Pat held me down.

What happened next was devastating to me. An ambulance came to the front of the school. Paramedics came in and took this kid away on a stretcher.

I thought I had my anger under control.

I didn't.

He went to the hospital and I went to the principal's office. I knew I was in a whole heap of trouble.

I wondered what Randy and Sonya would think?

What my social worker would think?

What the state would think?

Then something unexpected happened. Witnesses came forward. They told the principal what happened. They were honest. They said this other kid started the fight. I was not punished because I had been defending myself. The other boy was suspended for 10 days.

The next year, when we stared high school, I saw him again. This time it was on the football field.

Again something remarkable happened. We *bonded*. We became friends. He began to understand me. I began to understand him. I was a running back, he was a linebacker. When the season started I told the coach we needed him in the game to help block or knock over players on the other team. Together, along with the rest of our teammates, we took the Conner Cougar's to its first state championship playoff game in ten years. I set many records as running back with his support and tough-nosed play. Football and a common goal brought us together.

While Qwa'el and I were inseparable at school and on the weekends, our home life was dramatically different.

In many ways it was harder for me because I went home every afternoon to a white family. They loved me. I loved them. They had never dealt with racism. No one had ever called them "Nigger." They never faced racial bullying. They never got into a fight because of the color of their skin. They never had to deal with the stress of racism. They didn't understand how to handle these types of issues or advise me on how to deal with racists.

Some kids would pretend to be my friend or pretend to be Qwa'el's friend, then they would lie to us about the other. It was a subtle form of racism designed to put a wedge between us. Not knowing any better, Qwa'el and I would argue and I would sulk about it all weekend. Qwa'el's mom told him we needed to stick together. In the end, their lies brought us closer together.

And stick together we did.

Racism was worse in high school, mainly because we were noticing girls . . . and they were noticing us.

My white friends were dating. Qwa'el and I were also dating, but in secret.

Girls at our high school were unsure of what their parents and friends would say if they knew they liked a black kid. And for me, many of their parents also knew I was a foster child and believed I really didn't have a future.

If a girl liked us we couldn't go hang out at the mall or the movies, we had to get creative. We would invite girls over to a friend's house where it was safe.

Ian and Doug were two of our best friends in high school. They were white. Their parents never cared if we brought girls over. People would call Ian a "whigger." He was into hip hop music. He introduced me to NWA. Doug's parents treated me like I was their second son. Doug's mother even took Doug and me to Chicago when we were in the eighth grade. It was only the second time I had ever left the state of Kentucky.

Since Ian and Doug associated with Qwa'el and me, they were also the target of racist remarks and actions. There was a group of skinheads in Northern Kentucky in the 1990's. They wore Doc Martins and black jackets with "POW" patches and confederate flags. They also wore red shoelaces and suspenders. One day we got word they were looking for Doug. They had heard he was a friend of "Niggers." Doug and Ian suffered for our friendship. Doug, Ian and their families have my utmost respect and love.

With this whole dating issue I also found myself having long conversations with Qwa'el's parents. They understood racism. They had a point of reference about what I was going through. They were willing to confront racism head on, where my foster parents were much more passive, hoping not to rock the boat.

All this came to a head in the fall of 1991. My foster family and I were going through some serious family issues; their older son was having marital problems, their younger son was about to become a father, and their daughter, had relationship problems of her own as she transitioned into womanhood.

Randy, my foster father, left for Washington State for a temporary job with his company. I was pushing them to help me deal with the racial issues I was facing; to act as an advocate for me. Some of their extended family members had made comments to me about my "big lips" and "big nose." And a local pastor had told me how "God's word required me to marry my own kind." These issues stoked the fire within me. Sonya was left to hold down the fort with all of these competing issues.

It got to be too much. After living with Randy and Sonya for five and a half years, the news came. Sonya was going to leave Kentucky and move to Washington to live with Randy.

I was shocked.

I was mad.

And I was heartbroken.

How could Randy and Sonya just throw me away; throw away five and a half years of love and support?

How could I go back to East Lexington?

How could I go back to the projects?

How could I go back to abject poverty?

The state took me away from my family at eight. Were they going to send me back at sixteen?

Could I be the man of the house?

What would that entail?

Selling drugs? Stealing? Robbing? Prison? Death?

I had come so far. I was between two worlds. And I didn't see a way out.

The first person I told was Qwa'el. The look on his face said it all.

He asked why?

I told him Sonya was going to Washington to be with Randy. I did not have another foster home to go to.

He looked me in the eyes and said, "That's messed up, G . . . Messed up!"

I felt the same way. I said, "Maybe it's time for me to get back home and be the man my father never was."

We didn't talk much more about it. Instead we reminisced about the eighth grade when we danced to *My Prerogative* and made everyone laugh.

Mentally I was preparing for life back in East Lexington; living with a mother of five and on welfare.

Where would I play football?

Where would I go to school?

Where would I work?

I didn't sleep that night.

I thought about eating only one meal a day, wearing the same clothes two and three days a week and dealing with the giant roaches.

I had come so far, why did I deserve this?

Early the next morning I got up and went to school. All of these thoughts were still running through my mind. I was depressed and heartbroken. Qwa'el came up to me with this boyish grin on his face and hit me on my arm.

He says, "G, G, I have something to tell you."

I was not in a good mood. I growled, "What's wrong with you?"

He said, "I told my folks what was going on with you and they said they would be your foster parents!"

What??!!!

I paused for a second. I wanted him to say it again, because I wasn't sure I heard him correctly.

After a long second I asked, "What did you say?"

"You heard me! My mother and Hop (Qwa'el's Stepfather) said they would be your foster parents."

My soul burst open.

I did the only thing I knew to do; I started dancing. I was like a puppy wanting to play. But I needed to hear these words from his parents. Growing up as a kid in the system, I needed to hear confirmation from his parents; I needed that security.

The rest of my day was a blur. I paid no attention to my teachers. For once, I was very quiet in my classes that day. Thoughts of living with my best friend consumed me. I watched the seconds on the clock click by. It seemed like the day would never end.

The butterflies started about 3:00 pm. Ian drove us to Qwa'el's house. As we got closer I began to sweat. My mouth got very dry. My palms were sweaty. My shirt was wet. My heart felt like it would pound through my chest. Q's mom was home when we got there.

This was my moment of truth.

I walked in with my eyes wide open.

Their small home was filled with photos. Some included me. I took my hat off. I sat down on their couch.

Mrs. Harris came into the room. She had a smirk on her face.

She barely got out, "Hi George." before I asked, "Is it true? Are you and Mr. Harris going to be my new foster parents?"

She politely said, "Yes, it is true, if we qualify."

I didn't hear anything after 'Yes.' It was the security I needed. I was ecstatic. I stopped sweating. I got some water. I was able to breathe again.

After that day I didn't talk much to Sonya or any of their family. I was still somewhat disappointed they were leaving me.

I did what every foster kid does, I packed up and got ready to go to my new home. I remember taking down my pictures. There were so many memories. While I was excited to go live with the Harris family, there was sadness about leaving Randy, Sonya, April, Jeff and Abe… my first foster family.

I packed my black garbage bags.

I opened the door one last time.

Tears filled my eyes as I left that day.

My mind began to focus on my new home. There was a certain sense of stability and security. I showed up at Qwa'el's house with a wide grin on my face. That day my best friend became my brother.

It was October of 1991 when I first moved in with Qwa'el. His parents Melanie and Greg, or Money and

Hop as they were affectionately known, had been a part of my extended family for several years. From the time I walked through the door, I was treated the same as their other two children.

As I mentioned before, their elder son was named Larry. Qwa'el was their younger son. Education was a priority. I was expected to work hard, study and get good grades. Education came before sports. If I didn't excel in the classroom I would not get to play football.

Hop and Money sacrificed many days and nights attending foster parent training. Both worked second shift jobs. They had to get up early during the week and on the weekends. The training was mandatory and they had to complete it before the state would let them become foster parents. I had no idea about what was expected of them in order to become foster parents. I was just happy to have a new home.

Later they even considered adopting me. Even though I loved them, I would not let them. I felt like my past was in the East Side Projects of Lexington. If they adopted me it would take away my roots, where I was from and who I was. They respected my wishes and never questioned my decision.

Every evening Qwa'el and I worked on our dance routines. I became one of the dominate football players in Northern Kentucky, while Qwa'el became quite the basketball player. We were very proud of our African-American heritage. We wanted to be liked and appreciated not just for our athletic ability, but also for who we were personally. We wanted to break the stereotypes of black kids in an all-white community.

Me at 13. Football was a big part of
my teenage years.

My brother Monqwa'el, my cousin Nikki and me.

Hop, my biological mother, Money, me and My Angel

Comparison of the plaque I got from the Sports View with the one I got in the middle of the night from my High School.
Photo by Crimson Duvall.

My biological mom at my high school graduation. She was so proud.

Chapter 7
Football

By the time Qwa'el and I were freshmen in High School I was beginning to excel at football. I had put on about 20 pounds of muscle and I was very fast. I played running back.

Qwa'el, on the other hand, gave up football to focus on basketball. Even though we didn't play football together anymore we still were inseparable because we had many of the same classes.

My high school was proud of its sports history. If you walked the hallways you could see pictures of all the previous athletes who had made their mark; basketball, baseball, football, track and field, wrestling and others, each sport had pictures of their best athletes. If you looked through all of the pictures you would see a proud history of athletes who excelled. Student athletes who held state records were there as well as those who led their team to state championships.

Well, except for one. There were no pictures of Melvin Miles.

Melvin Miles held the single season rushing record.

He scored the most touchdowns in a single game.

He scored the most touchdowns in a single season.

He led the Cougars to their first and only state football championship in 1983.

To top it off, he was a great person.

Everyone compared me to Melvin. After my Junior season I set a goal for my Senior season: to break Melvin's records. It got me to wondering, *Where are Melvin Miles's photos? Where is his plaque? Where are his records?* I would find out soon.

After one football practice in the summer of my senior year, I went to get some rib pads from the equipment room. As I walked in I saw a large wall of boxes stacked from floor to ceiling with football pads and equipment.

It was going to take me awhile to find the rib pads.

As I moved the boxes around, I noticed some paintings on the back wall.

The wall was painted with statistics. . . Melvin Miles' statistics.

Why were his accomplishments covered by boxes in the equipment room, out of sight and out of the minds of the students, faculty and visitors?

Like me, Melvin Miles was black.

I went to my coach and asked him why Melvin Miles did not have any pictures up around the school like the other former athletes. He didn't know, he wasn't the coach in 1983.

I asked my coach, what are you going to do to make sure Melvin Miles gets the same recognition as white athletes.

He asked, "What do you want me to do about it?"

I told him I would like to see Mr. Miles picture up along the walls at Connor like all the other former white athletes. I wanted the students, faculty and visitors to know about the accomplishments of a black athlete who excelled. I wanted them to put a face with the stories. He was a big part of their football history and they should know he was a black athlete.

I used Miles' accomplishments on the football field as a blueprint for my personal hard work and success. I felt like I owed it Melvin Miles. To date Mr. Miles' picture still does not hang in the halls of Connor High

School. The wall listing his accomplishments in the equipment room has been painted over.

Even though I set or broke all of Melvin Miles's records, I received little recognition for my accomplishments. The same year I broke all those records, a white basketball player hit a last second shot to send the basketball team, which Qua'el played on, to the state tournament. T-shirts were printed and sold and his number was placed on the floor at the spot where he took the game-winning shot.

When I scored the winning touchdown in the game that sent our football team to the playoffs for the first time in ten years (the year Melvin Miles had been the running back) all I was told was, "Good job, George."

Many other organizations recognized my athletic accomplishments.

I was named co-player of the year by the *Cincinnati Enquirer*.

I won several player of the week awards from Sports View, a local channel covering high school football, Famous Recipe, and Coca-Cola.

Everyone was watching as they gave me this huge plaque with a big football in the middle. I knew the other students recognized my accomplishments as a football player. But my school gave me no special recognition.

Later my Coach told me they would put a plaque up in the hallway in my honor as the record breaker. But I had to do all the work. I would have to take the plaque order to a shop in Newport, Kentucky, a town about 20 miles away, along with one of my own personal photographs. Once it was finished I would have to go back to Newport and pick it up. Connor would pay for it and put it on display.

It seemed odd that I had to do all the work. I was somewhat confused, but if that is what it took for future Connor football players to see and recognize who held these records, it was worth it.

One day, I was even pulled out of one of my classes during school to receive the Player of the Year award from Sports View.

I got a plaque from my high school too. Money, my mother, gave it to me one night around midnight, after she got home from work. Someone from my high school gave it to a man who worked with my Mom and asked if she would give it to me. I pulled it out of the small plastic bag. It was about the size of my hand and it said:

Connor High School

1994 Record Breaker

George Duvall

2568 Yd's Rushing 26 TD's.

I was very disappointed, not because of the award, but in how it was given to me. I remembered the excitement around the school when the basketball team went to the state tournament and they sold t-shirts and put the kid's number on the floor. On the other hand, I got a plaque in the middle of the night. I thought it was because I was black.

I figured they wanted me behind the rib pad boxes with Melvin!

Chapter 8
Growing Up Black where Everyone Else is White

Adolescence is tough and stressful for most parents and their children. For me there was the added pressure of growing up black where everyone else was white. My adolescence dealt with normal teenage issues, but I was also dealing with racial issues and working through my own past. I've come to believe we all live in a fallen world. In many ways we are all broken people who are shaped by our experiences and perceptions. What follows is my perception of events and how they shaped my life and my view of foster care.

Call it what you will, most of America still struggles with diversity; whether it is black kids in white neighborhoods, white kids in black neighborhoods, kids with two moms or dads, Muslim kids in a Christian neighborhood or Christian kids in a Muslim neighborhood. No matter what the situation, minorities face bullying, discrimination and violence. Lots of people see and even understand the danger, but very few must live with it.

Early in foster care I learned to approach other people, especially authority figures with a positive attitude. I was a black foster child. I came from a place much different than everyone around me. I was acutely aware of my differences. In order to gain respect and trust I had to be a better version of myself. I was naturally extroverted, but I felt like I had to overcompensate for my blackness. I developed this ultra-positive attitude about life. I spent an unusual amount of time talking with my friend's parents. I wanted to let them know where I came from and how I turned my life around. Even though my background was very different from anything they encountered, my attitude and charisma usually won them over.

Except when it came to girls.

Earlier I mentioned how tough it was to have relationships with girls. On more than one occasion my heart was broken. Like many adolescent males I found girls irresistible. I had many secret crushes. Talking with them and flirting with them made my heart race. But deep down I knew no matter how charming I was, no matter how good I behaved, and no matter how much the girl liked me I had no chance.

Few parents wanted their young white girl to date a black dude.

Even with my athletic accomplishments, academic record, and charismatic attitude, I was a pariah when it came to dating.

My white friends were dating, why couldn't I?

What did "being black" have to do with anything?

My first secret crush began in the sixth grade. She was the one who told me blacks and whites shouldn't be together. Her mother told her it was in the Bible. She still liked me. We talked to each other for years in private. In public we tried not to show our interest in each other. She eventually moved on to high school as I entered junior high.

That relationship taught me how to break down barriers with girls.

I also developed a talent for talking like my white counterparts.

If I got a girl's phone number and wanted to call, I had to talk like a white guy. When I called a girl I could adjust my voice making it more high-pitched and enunciating every word like my white friends did. Usually it worked. Once the girl was on the phone I could go back to my normal voice.

In all honesty it was not safe to date girls at my school. Most of my relationships were secret, by necessity. The danger hit close to home when I was a junior in high school. It happened at one of my football games.

Qwa'el and I always supported each other. He came to all of my football games. I was safe on the football field and Qwa'el was usually safe in the stands, but this night was different. The game was in the third quarter. An older white man walked up into the stands near to where Qwa'el was sitting.

He asked, "Who is Monqwa'el?!"

Qwa'el stood up and said, "That's me."

The man looked him up and down. His face started turning red. His eyes squinted. He pulled a knife out and growled, "You better stay away from my daughter or I'm gonna kill you."

Qwa'el started turning white.

Luckily, a friend's father was nearby. His name was Gary.

Gary was white, and big. He jumped between the man and Qwa'el and told the man, "You have five seconds to get the hell outt'a here." The man didn't move.

Then Gary began to walk toward the man counting off, "One . . . Two . . . Three. . ."

The man turned and slinked away toward his car.

Gary told his son, Chris, to take Qwa'el to his apartment.

I had a great game that night, unaware that anything had gone on. After getting back to the locker room, I heard what had happened to Qwa'el. My stomach jumped up into my throat. I quickly changed clothes and went to look for him.

I didn't even take a shower.

I wanted to make sure my brother was safe.

One of my friends drove me back to my house. Qwa'el wasn't home.

I called Hop to let him know what happened.

He asked where Qwa'el was.

I didn't know.

All I knew was he left the football field with Chris. I didn't know if the guy followed them. I didn't know who the guy was. I didn't know if he was really dangerous.

Hop said in his scratchy strained voice "Keep your ass at the house until I get home."

I did.

When Hop got home we hopped into his little black Chevette and headed towards Chris' father's apartment. This was before cell phones became popular and affordable.

On the way over Hop grilled me about Qwa'el, the girl he was dating, and her father.

Hop told me we had to be careful dating white girls because of situations like this.

Finally, we got to Chris' apartment. We knocked on the door. No one answered.

Hop asked if I knew where the girl's father lived. I knew if he found this girl's father things would get much more complicated.

I convinced him to go back to our house first and see if Qwa'el had gotten home.

When we got back to our house Qwa'el was there. I felt somewhat relieved.

He explained what happened to Hop. And he explained it again when Money got home.

After we went to bed, Qwa'el confided to me he was scared to death when this girl's father approached him with a knife.

The man told Qwa'el "I love my daughter. I will kill someone over her. I advise you to stay away from her!"

After this incident Qwa'el told me how he was going to quit going out with white girls. I felt the same way. I didn't want to fight some girl's father or her extended family. Football became my girlfriend.

After that night before and after games we made sure we knew where the other one was and planned to stick together for our own safety.

Money and Hop had a long talk with us. Their oldest son, Larry, had dealt with similar situations. They told me to be careful. I had to make sure it was safe to date a girl of a different race; I needed to use my head and be aware of my surroundings. It made me mad. Other kids had no problems with dating or romantic relationships. Why did it have to be such an issue for me?

Their son, Larry, had a friend named Rodney. I called him Rod. He had graduated from the same high school a few years earlier and they thought it would be a good idea for us to meet. They were right. We immediately hit it off and he became my mentor. Rod was a light skinned black me. He was educated. He was smart. And he knew how to fish. We spend many evenings and weekends talking and fishing. He taught me a lot.

Blackness is great.

Never start trouble.

Learn your history.

Be a man. Not a punk.

Get an education. No one can take it away.

Plan ahead. You will have difficult situations. Prepare yourself.

Play Chess with life. Not Checkers.

I knew if I ever needed *anything* I could call Rod.

I took his advice to heart. I started studying black history in my spare time. Rosa Parks, Rev. Martin Luther King, Jr., Malcolm X. Their struggles. Their victories. Their history. It was my history.

My football coach was an advanced placement history teacher. One February he gave me a set of videotapes called *Eyes on the Prize*. These were videos showing the struggle of black Americans in the 50's, 60's and 70's. There were scenes showing African Americans getting beaten, bitten by dogs and sprayed with fire hoses in the South. It was a nice gift. He knew I was into black history.

However, I wondered, *Why he didn't show these videos to his history class?*

Why did he give them to one of the few blacks in the school?

Was he afraid of offending his white students?

Northern Kentucky was one of the last stops a slave made before freedom through the Underground Railroad. Did his students understand the significance?

Don't get me wrong, he may never have contemplated these issues, but given my circumstances I could not avoid them.

In foster care and in Northern Kentucky, I felt like I had to overcompensate for my blackness. Or I had to hide it. Most of my classmates or teachers were good people, but they never saw things through my eyes. They never faced the issues I faced. Randy and Sonya were good people, but it was difficult for them to see the world through my eyes. Hop and Money and Rod were intimately familiar with these issues. They were able to teach me appropriate responses. No matter what I did or didn't do, my blackness would have an effect on people. It just did because I was different. I stuck out.

When issues about my blackness came up at school I learned to address it head on, whether it was with friends, other students, or even teachers. How could I expect other people to understand my perspective if I didn't try to educate them? One event stands out.

In 1992 the movie, *Malcolm X*, hit theatres, and merchandise hit the stores. I bought a black shirt with a white X emblazoned across the chest. One day I wore it to school. That same day another kid wore a shirt with the Confederate Flag emblazoned on across the chest.

At the bottom of his shirt it said "You Wear Your X and I'll Wear Mine."

Of course I confronted him. I wanted to explain why I wore the Malcolm X shirt and how I found his shirt offensive.

The confederate flag is a sign of persecution and slavery to African Americans. The African slave trade dehumanized and destroyed millions upon millions of Africans. They were kidnapped from their homeland and transported to America–under such horrific conditions many died. At best they faced horrible working conditions. At worst, they were physically abused, sexually abused, tortured and killed. Frederick Douglass, a leader of the abolitionist movement wrote this about his owner:

> "He was a cruel man, hardened by a long life of slave-holding. He would at times seem to take great pleasure in whipping a slave. I have often been awakened at the dawn of the day by the most heart-rending shrieks of an own aunt of mine, whom he used to tie up to

a joist and whip . . . til she was literally covered with blood. No words, no tears, no prayer, from his gory victim seemed to move his iron heart from its bloody purpose."[*]

When I saw the confederate flag I saw slave masters, not southern pride. Before anything could happen we both wound up in the principal's office. I explained to the principal why I wore the shirt and how it represented self-empowerment. I also taught the principal about Malcolm X and how he was a positive role model for black kids... Rod's mentoring had rubbed off on me.

The principal listened, but felt both t-shirts represented what he called "negativity." He ordered both of us to turn our shirts inside out for the rest of the day and go back to class. Then he said not to wear those shirts to school again.

I was confused.

How could Malcolm X represent "negativity"? He fought racism.

---

[*] Frederick Douglass, *The Narrative of the Life of Frederick Douglass* (Mineola, NY: Dover Publications, 1995), 3-4.

The Confederate flag represented oppression and enslavement of the black race; the Ku Klux Klan and lynching. How could he compare Malcolm X to the Confederacy? I was angry as I turned my shirt inside out and headed back to class.

As you can see it was hard for me to grow up in a predominately white community. I stood out while I wanted desperately to fit in. I overcompensated in sports and in school. I became as white as I could at times so authority figures would learn to trust me. I learned a lot about myself and what I could do.

I see the kids who stick out.

I empathize with them.

I am drawn to them.

I know their struggle.

It was mine.

Chapter 9
Foster Care 101

At 7 I was told by my uncle I would be dead or in prison by the time I was 13. My family also taught me the term D.T.A (DON'T TRUST ANYBODY) but yourself! Unfortunately, it made me an insecure foster child.

Thanks to my experience in foster care I finally learned to trust people; to see the good in others.

As a foster child you deal with a lot of separation both from your biological family, and from your friends.

You move from home to home.

You move from one foster family to another.

Social workers come and go on a regular basis.

They all claim everything will be ok.

Sometimes it's not ok.

Sometimes you are angry and want to scream.

Sometimes you are sad and want to cry.

Sometimes you just want to run away from it all.

The worst thing about growing up in the child welfare system is the nagging insecurity. You don't know who to trust. You don't know who to believe in. Even when you find a family who loves you, they may have no way of relating to you or what you go through.

Randy and Sonya were a great, loving family. They have a special place in my heart. Nevertheless, they were not black, they did not grow up in foster care. They did not grow up as a racial minority. And it affected our relationship.

Spending my high school years with Qwa'el, Larry, Money, Hop and my cousin Nikki, who came to live with us the summer before our junior year of high school, was a tremendous relief for my soul. Qwa'el and I started as friends and ended up brothers. Our relationship was sealed by the fire of racial tension.

I have often wondered why I deserved the life I got.

I came from nothing.

I entered foster care as a thief, a thug and a liar.

The world revolved around what I wanted, when I wanted it.

I agree with my uncle. I was headed for prison or the grave by the time I was 13.

But God intervened.

My punishment turned out to be a blessing.

My rage turned to love.

I saw a lot of wrong in East Lexington. So when I tasted the sweetness of the love that was available to me, from Randy and Sonya and then Money and Hop, I knew it was right.

Randy and Sonya took a risk. White parents taking in a black kid from the streets and bringing me to Rural Kentucky was risky. They showed me love has no color.

Qwa'el took a risk. He asked his family to take a chance on a foster kid; a former robber, thief and general thug.

Money and Hop took a risk, thinking they could make a difference in the life of a black kid adopted into a white community.

What these people did for me is indescribable.

They taught me to first love myself and to stop letting foster care be an excuse for me not to succeed in life, second to love others and third to love education.

People can take away your money, they can take away your things, but they can't take away your education.

Since I grew up without a father I knew once I had a child he or she would never have to worry about who their father was. I will never leave them.

Much like my Angel never left me.

My Angel and I on my fist trip outside of Kentucky. I was 13.

My Angel and I after one of my football
games in Northern Kentucky.

My Angel and I at my college graduation.

Chapter 10
My Angel

Angel - "A person of exemplary conduct or virtue." –
Author Unknown

At three, I was placed into a local daycare center. All of the children were from low income families. Never the shy kid, sometimes I walked into the director's office and started talking. The director was a petite white lady.

She actually listened and responded to what I had to say.

After talking for a while she would tell me, "OK George, it's time to go back to your room."

She smiled a lot. She had a lot of influence in Lexington. Little did I know how much she would influence my life.

Sometimes if there was an issue or problem with me or my family she would drive me from daycare back to my home to the East Side projects . . .

By herself.

It was unheard of for a white person, especially a petite white woman, to drive through the East Side. Then she would stay with me in the hood until my mother or someone she trusted showed up.

She knew my family history.

She knew where I was headed.

Yet, she still hovered over me for years.

Many of the other kids who crossed her path were no different than me. Why did she give me this attention? Many years later I asked her "Why me?"

Her answer was blunt, yet funny. "George, you just looked pitiful."

She continued "but you had interests and you were able to hold a conversation with me about President Jimmy Carter (who was President at the time) when you were just five years old. I knew you just needed a little extra help to make it in life."

She motivated me to escape my past and change my future.

In the summer, sometimes she would let me stay at her house for the weekend. I loved spending time with her at her home. I felt like a prince. She always had good food. She had cable television. And there was a lake behind her house where I could fish. The East Side and Foster Care was the furthest thing from my mind when I was there. She poured her life into me knowing I was a liar, a thief and a robber.

Her whole family was amazing.

Her sons showed me how to play ping pong. No one in the East Side projects played ping pong. I doubted they even knew what it was. I was very competitive and soon I was the house champion in the boy's facilities where I lived.

Her sons and I went fishing together at the lake behind their house. We became good friends. Years later her youngest son, Shawn, would make a trip to Northern Kentucky to watch me play football.

Anytime I knew there was someone in the stands from Lexington I played better. When he visited I had an awesome game.

I called her husband "Doc." He loved my energy and the way I danced. He was a biologist at the University of Kentucky. And he is from India. After dinner he would move the kitchen table out of the way and say with a typical Indian accent, "Come on George, show me your moves! Do it again! That's a good one!" We all smiled when my performance was over.

I felt valued when I was with her family.

She and her husband took me on my first trip outside of Kentucky. I was thirteen at the time. She, Doc and I flew to New Orleans to see their son who was attending Tulane University.

There were multiple times when she would drive from Lexington, an hour and a half away, to Northern Kentucky to pick me up and take me back to Lexington. She would then drive me back to Northern Kentucky and then spend another hour and a half driving herself back to Lexington.

One day, on the trip from Northern Kentucky to Lexington, she said, "You know you can go to college right?"

I replied, "That's what folks are saying. Football has been a blessing to me."

"I know you care about football, but I don't." She emphasized, "Football will end someday. What I'm saying is you can go to college if you want to."

"You think so?" I asked.

"I know so George. I would not be telling you this if I did not feel it was true."

"Even if I wanted to go to college, I don't think I can afford it."

"If you really want to go to college, I'll help you find a way to pay for it. Football will end and will be taken away from you. No one can ever take your education away."

Then I knew. I had no reason to fail.

She has been the most consistent person in my life.

She knew I was a robber and a thief.

She could have given up on me.

She didn't.

I wish every child in foster care had an angel; someone who would give them a second/third/fourth chance to become a better, more productive member of society. We all need second, third and fourth chances to succeed, especially foster children. Just when we learn to trust someone they leave or we are moved to another home or there is some other crisis. Foster children just want to belong. When I was with My Angel I always felt like I belonged.

Anytime she calls, no matter what I have going on, I take her call. If she *ever* needs me, I will be there.

My Angel was not influenced by trends or popular culture. She was eating organic before eating organic was cool, but I loved fast food, especially Burger King. Whenever she brought me home to visit my biological family, we would end up eating at Burger King because it was where I wanted to eat. Now I cannot pass a Burger King sign without thinking of her.

I think of her often.

When I got to college I wrote her a letter.

> Dear (Angel),
>
> Let me first start off by saying thank you. Thank you for everything that you have done for my family and me. You and your family have given me and my family hope and guidance towards our lives and my future.
>
> When I was just three years old, you took me into your school and taught me simple things a little kid should know. And at that point at your school, we

both bonded to each other not knowing that would change our lives forever. As time went on, no matter the situation, you and your family has been there to comfort me.

As I got a little older, I started to find myself getting in trouble. Now, most people would cut off a relationship with a trouble maker, but you were always there. You even let me stay at your home. Knowing that I was a thief and a con. You trusted me around you and your family's worldly goods. I thank you for that. After that, because you trusted me, I began to trust others more.

When I was taken away from my home and sent 90 miles away you and your family were there. Supporting me and watching my every move, as well as my families. By this time I was growing up. I'm starting to see life more clearly. Still you were there to give me congratulations and hope. Thank you. There were times when I thought I wasn't going to make it, but every time I did, I thought of you, Paul, Shawn and (Doc) and I knew that I would make it.

You were the first one to take me on a plane, the first to take me out of the state of Kentucky and the first to greet me when I graduated (high school). Thank you.

Every Christmas you have sent me gifts. Every Birthday you have called or made some kind of acknowledgement to let me know you are thinking about me. And I on the other hand have never given you anything. Thank you.

For many years I have been wanting to tell you how I feel about your family. Thank you guys for everything that you have done. I have always considered myself lucky, because not many kids are lucky to have three families. That's what I feel when I am around you and your family; a member or another son. I have considered you more as a mother than a friend.

Words cannot tell the true feelings I feel. But, I could not go on in life not letting you and your family know that , everything you have done, the knowledge that you have instilled upon me, and everything you have done for my family was not in vain.

I am in college and on my way to a bright future. I just wanted you to know that part of that is because of you and your family. Please share this letter with the others, so they can know they are in my heart.

I will make something of myself someday and let you and the other people in my life know that a big part was because of their support.

God bless you and your family, and please continue to monitor my progress.

Thank you

/s/ George E. Duvall

So Angel, here I am finishing my first book. Without you and your family, it would not be possible. Thank you again for the love and support you gave me. Thank you for all the sacrifices you made to save my life . . . to make sure I was not dead or in prison by the time I was thirteen.

I'm gonna' keep on Living Forward.

The end . . . for now.

CPSIA information can be obtained
at www.ICGtesting.com
Printed in the USA
FSHW011505301218
54478FS